First published 2025 by Macmillan Children's Books
an imprint of Pan Macmillan
The Smithson, 6 Briset Street, London, EC1M 5NR
Associated companies throughout the world
www.panmacmillan.com

ISBN 978-1-0350-7491-4

Text and illustration copyright © Macmillan Publishers International Ltd 2025

This book is not authorized, licensed or endorsed by Lionel Messi or any affiliate.

All rights reserved. No part of this publication may be reproduced, stored in a retrieval system, or transmitted, in any form, or by any means (electronic, mechanical, photocopying, recording or otherwise) without the prior written permission of the publisher. Any person who does any unauthorized act in relation to this publication may be liable to criminal prosecution and civil claims for damages.

2 4 6 8 9 7 5 3 1

A CIP catalogue record for this book
is available from the British Library.

Printed in China

EU representative: 1st Floor, The Liffey Trust Centre,
117-126 Sheriff Street Upper, Dublin 1 D01 YC43

Let's Meet MESSI

ILLUSTRATED BY GERALDINE RODRÍGUEZ
WRITTEN BY CATHERINE SAUNDERS

MACMILLAN CHILDREN'S BOOKS

On 24th June 1987 in Rosario, a city in Argentina, Jorge Messi and Celia Cuccittini celebrated the birth of their new baby boy.

They called him Lionel, which means 'young lion' — or Leo, for short.

Leo had two big brothers who loved playing football on the streets near their house.

As soon as he could walk, Leo joined in. Although he was the smallest, Leo was soon the best player!

Leo was happiest when he was playing football. He was really fast and scored lots of goals, usually with his left foot.

His brothers called him 'la pulgita', which means 'little flea' in Spanish, because he was small and strong.

At the age of four, Leo joined his first ever team, Grandoli. His grandmother often took him to matches and watched him play.

She was his biggest fan and Leo loved to make her feel proud.

When Leo started school, he played football in all his breaks. Everyone wanted to be on his team because it meant that they would probably win the match!

Leo dreamt of being a professional footballer when he grew up. When he was just six years old, his local team, Newell's Old Boys, asked him to play for their youth team.

Leo was quite shy, but playing football made him feel confident. In his first game for Newell's Old Boys, he scored four goals.

His team didn't lose a match for three years!

When he was about 10 years old, doctors told Leo that he needed some special expensive medicine to help his body grow.

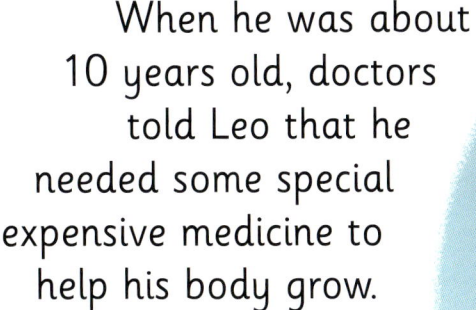

Luckily, FC Barcelona, one of the biggest football clubs in the world, offered to help him with his treatment if he joined them.

Leo missed the rest of his family, but he made lots of good friends at the FC Barcelona training academy.

When they weren't playing football, they liked to play video games together… about football!

At just 16 years old, Leo played his first game for Barcelona's main team. His dream of becoming a professional footballer had come true!

He couldn't wait to play with some of the best and most well-known footballers in the world.

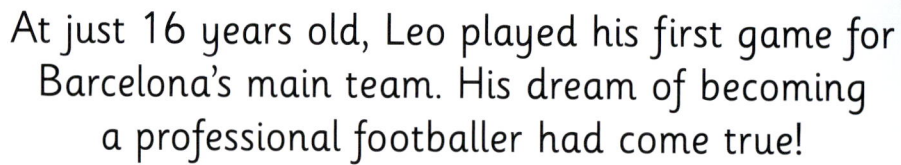

Leo played brilliantly and soon he was famous all over the world too.

Leo was 18 years old when he began playing for his country, Argentina. Seeing him in the famous blue and white shirt made Leo's family so proud.

A few years later, Leo became Argentina's captain. It was a big responsibility, but he was ready to be a leader on the pitch.

Off the pitch, Leo was a great friend to his teammates. He was also a superstar footballer with millions of fans!

But life wasn't all about football for Leo. With his wife Antonela, he had three sons. He loved being a dad even more than he loved playing football!

Leo felt very lucky. It made him want to help other people, too.

He set up his own charity, the Leo Messi Foundation, to help children all around the world.

All around the world, children looked up to Leo. They tried to copy his ball skills and wore shirts with his name and number on.

Although Leo had won many trophies with his clubs, there was still something he hoped to win – a trophy for Argentina!

As captain, Leo had to inspire his team. He encouraged them to try as hard as they could and to never give up.

Finally, Argentina triumphed at the Copa América, a South American football tournament.

Now, there was just one more important trophy Leo wanted to win for his country, the World Cup.

Leo had played in four World Cups with Argentina and lost two finals. Although it had been heartbreaking, he was determined that his fifth World Cup would be different.

Even after Argentina lost their first game, Leo was still sure they could win.

He inspired his teammates to really believe in themselves... and they did it! Leo and his squad became World Cup winners at last!

Now Leo had won more trophies than any other footballer before him, but he wasn't ready to stop playing football yet.

Lots of clubs wanted him to play for them, but he chose to move to Inter Miami, in America.

Leo was keen to share his skills with new fans, and show them why he thinks football is the best game in the world.

Leo trains a lot to keep his skills sharp and his body fit and strong. He knows that being a footballer is hard work — but it's worth it!

Leo loves to bring joy to his fans, especially children. He always makes time to sign autographs or pose for photos.

When he's not playing for his team, Leo likes to hang out with his family and friends, and even play some football!

Many people think that so far, Leo is the greatest footballer ever. Maybe that's why he's been voted the best player in the world an incredible eight times.

But that's not the most important thing to Leo.
He just loves playing football!

When he has the ball at his feet, he still feels like that happy little boy playing on the streets of Rosario.